The Iniscarra Bar
and Cycle Rest

Dillons Sept '95

To Gehenie
with lots of love

from Martha

Martina Evans

The Iniscarra Bar and Cycle Rest

Rockingham Press

Published in 1995
by
The Rockingham Press
11 Musley Lane,
Ware, Herts
SG12 7EN

British Library Cataloguing-in-Publication Data

A catalogue record for this book
is available from the British Library

ISBN 1 873468 32 6

Printed in Great Britain
by Bemrose Shafron (Printers) Ltd,
Chester

Printed on Recycled Paper

For Declan and Líadain

Acknowledgements

Some of the following poems appeared first in the pages of *Ambit, Camden Voices, Cobweb, Dog, Endless Mountain Review (U.S.), Fat Chance, Hybrid, Iota, New Virago Poets, New Hope International, The Observer, Poetry Ireland Review, Poetry Nottingham, The Bound Spiral, The Independent, The New Statesman and Society, The Rialto, The Sunday Tribune, Smith's Knoll, Spokes, Smoke, Seam, The Third Half, What Poets Eat, Vision On 1994* and *The Wide Skirt*. I am grateful to the editors concerned. And special thanks to my sister, Mary, for all her help and encouragement.

Contents

Section 1: Flying over Burnfort Cross   9
The Good Witch   10
Favourites   11
Hurts   12
Trickster Moon   13
Soft Talk   14
Dangerous Talk   15
Two Cows   16
Time for Serpent and Cow   17
Donkey   18
Island Grave   19
Star over France   20
Puck Fair   21
Cow and Calf   22
Harvest Moon   23

Section 2: "Got on a lucky one ..."   24
The Boy who could Talk   25
Stretch me   26
Mapping   27
Remember Iniscarra Graveyard 1983   28
Dispatch   29
Waking   30
Jaunty   31
The Ear   32
How your disappointments affect me   33
Kiss   34
Hearts   35

Section 3: The heart of Holloway   36
The King of the Talkers   37
Holloway Road Nocturne   38
Here Comes Summer   39
Edge   40
Still   41
The Silent Type   42

Winter   43
Messenger   44
The Air   45
Satsumas   46
To Toblerone   47
Missing Mountains   47
The Plain Speaker   48
Not Rumpelstiltskin   49

    Section 4: "Love set you going ..."   50
Labour in October   51
Winter's Grip   52
Falling   53
Sleep   54
This Passion   55
Separating   56
Wake   57
Knitting   58
Insomnia   59
Liadain's Gloves   60
Blue Frost Moon   61

    Section 5: Like a coloniser   62
Gale   63
Ward A 11   64
Barium Swallow   65
There's a Snake in my Back   66
Ghosts   67
Revision of a Hip Replacement   68
Good Killers   69
Crocodile   70

    Section 6: "Come then, royal girl ..." 72
Like an Angel from Below   73
The Blank Map   74
The Curse   75
Nancy's Mirror   76
Dyeing   77
Loves' Kitchen   78
Her Lesson   79
Dear Mother   80

Section 1:

Flying over Burnfort Cross

Hurts

Picking berries
on the Island Road
in July
hurts we called them.

Digging our teeth into
the little pains
of berries
and the blood bursting
out of them.

They were whortleberries really.

It was sweet in July
picking hurts on the Island Road
just being and eating
not planning or storing up
and returning home with an empty jam jar
stomachs full of hurts in July.

Trickster Moon

The Island road is white tonight,
the Virgin Mary rushed past the graveyard
I'm hiding and lost in the big woods
singing Kevin Barry was no coward
while the cows that I think
are mad staring bulls
assault me with their curiosity

I must break the green of Deane's field
sow the fields and cocks of hay.
Unpick the badness that dropped over me
on a full fool moon night.

Soft Talk

The politicians had soft talk
and soft palms to rub it in with.
The people kind of liked it too.
Liked being courted.
Liked to toss their heads and say,
Well I'd never turn my back on Dev...
Sink their suddenly valuable lips
into a free pint of Guinness.
Or throw back a fiery nip
of Powers Gold Label whiskey.
Heady nights.
We'll take care of you, boy!
Talk of government grants,
planning permission,
and jobs in the Civil Service.
The End of Emigration.
A smoky hum massing under the low ceiling
from men with toupees, tinted glasses
and briefcases, who knew Dublin and hotels
and women who drank Martinis.
Men who weren't afraid to shake
hands scented with diesel or manure
on the nights coming up to the election.

Dangerous Talk

The boys were building walls in the woods,
the girls had briar scratches right up
to the top of their short skirts.
1973. The teachers were talking politics.

The children dipped and floated among the evergreens,
folded their hands around dry cones,
lay on beds of soft brown needles,
smoked Major Extra Strong.

The sensible and the anxious returned often to check
the sixteen paned grey windows where the Master and Miss
opened and shut their mouths, sealed behind glass and stone.
Finally, reports about kissers, smokers,

and seven heads bobbing on top of tombstones
prevailed upon the priest. A shy man, it was hard
on him having to snorkel down to the school and deliver
the two breathless victims from their pressured cabin.

Two Cows

Tonight in the
black field,
two cows
have their backs
to the graveyard
their creamy thick
bodies
straining the breeze.

Two cows,
you carry
our story
with your mouths
chewing and sulky
your heads
white and curly
in the iron wind
that blows over
from the bleached
headstones.

Time for Serpent and Cow

Dead will be those
who crushed the upright serpent
and the eye of the cow
will glisten brown and warm
in the beauty of it's chosen fertility
when the men
in the black frocks
who beat
the bounty of our women
with their blackthorn sticks
must know
it's closing time.

Donkey

And my arms around
your leathery back
knowing the tragedy
of silence,
the moisture in your eyes,
the pain in your
uncut hooves,
the finity
of a length of rope
And only your
sad savage screech
to punctuate
the tragedy in your silence.

Island Grave

At the Passage Grave at Island,
a scythe wind scraped the grey sky.
It was May month,
the old month of enforced chastity
and the unlucky hawthorns
pointed to the passage grave,
two cremated bodies within
and one without.
Who were the lucky ones
we wondered.

Teddy roared at the cows
while Mary was filling her arms
with Thistle and Weed,
and
the cows roared back
as they skirted the grave
on the way to the milking parlour.

Star over France

A sheep turned his back,
the baby buzzard swung
on his high nest
over the black quietness
of the sleeping poppies,
and
a bright star stopped and shone.

You stayed out
to watch the sky,
wine filled and mystic,
while I was chiselled
with fright in the hush.
As soon as I could,
I fled the field
afraid the Virgin Mary
would appear from that bright
planet, bellying out
her blue cloak at me,
her pink cheeks blooming,
charging me with sin.

Puck Fair

After all these
years of Patrick, saints
and Moving Marys,
they still crown a goat
king in Killorglin
a goat, scalded and cross,
crowned and mounted
to survey the
tinkers, horse dealers,
drinkers
and three card trick men.

'Twas the night of Scattering
Day, that the young boy, passing
Droumavalla graveyard, heard
Would you ever give us a
hand over,
stricken and lost,
the voice of a drunk who'd
got lost from the fair.

Or so his aunt said,
nursing her ninth child,
born on the eleventh day of
that porter driven month,
alone at the farmhouse,
except for the shivering
boy, she had little time for
ghosts.

Cow and Calf

I heard the cow
lowing in the wet
evening, the grass
criss-crossed on
our wellingtons,
the rain
raising smells
from our hair.

Ah calf, calf,
they pulled you
away from me after
all my hard work,
after you emerged
hair wet slicked.
I go now in pain,
my bony knees shuddering
my udders heavy,
on down the
boreen, under the stick
of the man that minds me
to the machine that
will release me.

Mammy, mammy,
I'm the calf
you licked before
they took me away
from you,
to the dark hold
that cuts across
the breaking sea

Boreen = laneway (Irish)

22

to the crate
where they'll mind me,
standing room for one,
milk but not yours,
for months,
till I'm ready.

Harvest Moon

How round, how yellow
was the moon that night,
when it bowled across
the secret blue sky.

How peculiar, how beamy
was the moon as we came
by the mountain road
at eleven o'clock.

How near, how low
was the moon beside us,
nudging the ditches
all the way from Killavullen.

How human, how reckless
seemed the moon, pitching
a low line along the
brave bowl of the sky.

We couldn't talk,
so clear was the night
and the air bearing down
on the black ditches.

Section 2:

"Got on a lucky one, came in eighteen to one."
Shane MacGowan, *Fairy Tale of New York.*

The Boy who could Talk

His head was shaved,
it was like a black sweet,
he rode the comedy bicycle,
head in the wind, legs on fire,
black hair, white face,
black jacket, short cuffs,
white wrists, made me
laugh naked pelvis deep
in bed. All night,
till six o'clock the following evening,
my room was lit up with the moon
of his Pan Face. There was no day and no time.
And no lecture halls. I didn't need
lectures when he made me laugh,
I was with the boy who could talk.

Stretch me

Stretch me and
I'll stretch you
We'll cover the world
together
boy of a hundred chocolates
Milky bar of my young days.

I see you forever
dancing blackly in your wedding suit
and I'm sweet with thinking
of how I solemnly tripped with you.

Mapping

Under Saint Finbarr's Cathedral
you asked me to marry you
and the golden angel
sneered indulgently.
We were wild with excitement
and we mapped it all over
Cork City.

From Barrack Street to the Teach Beag
Maria Domus to Jo's Caff,
your feet in Doc Marten's,
mine in yellow boats
drunk with kissing
and Woodpecker cider,
making criss-cross lines
for colouring in the boxes
in the after years.

Remember Iniscarra Graveyard 1983

I can see the pub door
where we leaped over the
wrestling hens, and where
the aproned old woman
served men in leather
jackets, while the juke box
boiled up Country & Western,
But I can't remember the
graveyard. Just us, feeling
joined in the old ruined
tower, rain dropping down
from the hole in the roof.

Too romantic, we said
afterwards, over our pints,
cynical students
nestling our knees
under the hard rocky
tables and dodging the cues
of the pool players in the
Iniscarra Bar & Cycle Rest.

Dispatch

For Declan

A thin curl of moon is lying
on her back over the red barn church,
a crown of snow sits hard on the roof.
Nudging into the blue black night,
the road is slippy,
I'm driving slow,
afraid to breathe,
afraid I'll die,
afraid of the cup going from my lips,
before my cold fingers let me through
the white flaked doorway,
up the shivered stairs,
to click into the flat
and drop my stiff coat.
Before I can run into our orange room
with my red face
and my fat pocket of good news.

Waking

Well into your skin,
waking
I feel your body,
sodden with sleep,
same as mine.
In the night,
our cells exchanged,
now we adhere,
your face bound
to my shoulder
the closeness laid down
at night
fusing one web of skin
that stretches
as we yawn and pull
the covers,
then separate for the short
run to get to the baby's room.

Jaunty

Light strikes the clock!
I've waited five hours
for you to come
crashing in
apologising,
kissing my feet,
and jaunty.

Jaunty! I'll give you
jaunty, I've waited,
while my mouth dried up,
a wrinkled raisin of fear,
saw the crash,
put you in the ambulance,
attended the funeral,
bawled at the grave,
comforted the orphan,
collected the insurance,
all these long
clock ticking hours,
till you came in,
apologising,
kissing my feet,
and jaunty.

The Ear

A malicious snip
in the bar
that evening
worked its way
under the skin,
slowly fizzing
as the night wore on,
blew up in the taxi,
shoved us from seat
to seat, until
without his knowing
the back of the taximan's
head turned into an ear.
A huge listening ear,
kind but firm
winking and wagging,
brightening through the glass
as our words died down.
We put up our tent,
passed the pipe,
located the jealous sprite
in the story, no we would
not separate, not us,
we couldn't, not us,
us with our two red hearts
burning fierce.

How your disappointments affect me

A handful of words
gathered,
shape themselves into
the top of a small
pointed spade,
which inserted
beneath the skin
under the rib cage,
draws the water
of tears
from my side.

Your disappointments hurt me.

Kiss

The bluebells swam around
the birch legs, making an indigo
smoke blanket that ran down
the slope, a witchy blue light,
that charmed the air
and made it ravenous.
Matching the knot in my back
to the gnarl of an oak,
I pressed hard, bringing pain
closer. Honeysuckle hearts hammered,
your warm tongue was in my mouth,
pushing Spring
and the primrose ditch
shifted and quaked inside of me.

                    Somerset, 22nd April 1993

Hearts

In cartoons, they jut out and pump,
stretching the skin of victims,
thump, thump, perfect symmetries,
Christmas colours, cellophane wrapped.

They can be stones or broken.
Or forgotten. On X-rays their curves
are shy, veering to one side.
Like that arrow I got.

I could no more have plucked it out
than I could have stopped the sky
peeling the morning you sent me
your old overcoat in the post.

Section 3:

The heart of Holloway

The King of the Talkers

He's the king of the talkers,
leaning forward to light his cigarette,
he'll give you a shrewd look.
Is it that that does it?
Because you feel he knows it all.

But laughter he deals that out too,
until laughing like a maniac
you fall drunk, nailed to his talk.
He's good for nothing only talk, said his mother
who could never get enough of him.

Holloway Road Nocturne

It was you,
you Paddy
stepping it out
of the Cock Tavern
of a night
who greeted
a nervous poet
mumbling verse
in a blue cape
with,
Well Bejaysus Hup!
You're like a wasp.

A red wasp,
thought the poet
immediately
flattered by the
descriptive greeting
in the dark.

A new poem,
thought the poet
greedily
turning the cape
down a sidestreet.

Here Comes Summer

The light
is increasing,
a pale blue
washes in gently,
welcome replacement
for the orange
and black city madness
that reigned
all winter. If I saw
that it was good,
I would swallow
the host that sticks
in my throat.
But I see next August,
a pit of hot concrete,
while I heave
heavy bags from Sainsbury's
my head surmounted
by infernal air
picking my way
through the gapes
in the pavement,
and the beer drenched fiends
outside J.J. Moons of Holloway.

Edge

Landseer Road is beating, it's heart
caged in the white house on the corner.
Mad rag rap music is pacing, pounding,
raging to get out. Heat hangs in the air.
Haven't you lost your virginity yet?
an eleven year old asks her sunglassed companion.
Time to go in, I say, with school marm lips
and carry my daughter off in an armful.
I fumble with the front door lock
and a Galway man stops to say, *Ye can all
feck off with yerselves.* He wheels away
in a dusty lurch. A wind blows and the trees
shut down their leaves, this street
is drawing arcs on the edge of madness.

Still

Above our square, the world
is round and the moon visits.
Below, I rest my aching back
against the boot of our car
and tilt upwards. Blue green leaves
glow copper at the edges,
the big blue above broods deep
and timeless, right and round,
yes, I can still ascend,
yes, after supper,
on the crest of my coffee,
I can still ascend,
even after the man with the yellow
eyes and the thin lips whipped
his wife with the word *prostitute*
and ran roaring crying across the park.

The Silent Type

I always wanted
to be
the silent type
wisdom welling
from my pores,
sitting quietly
perusing
brooding
on the problems
of others
never a word
about myself
of course.
Just once in
a while, uttering
a carved sentence,
round, universal,
eternal,
savagely biblical,
heavy
on the heads
of gossips,
sending them scurrying
from the bellow and blaze
of my thunder and lightning.

Winter

Ice cracked wings
on the windscreens,
balls of white wind
at your mouth,
frozen features clamp
the smile off your face,
you're afraid to wonder
where the tramp
with the white iced coat
slept last night.

Cover the baby's head
with muffling wool caps,
stand in front to keep
the fog from her face,
block the wind that blows
down from the tower block,
crush her in your arms,
mightily.

And yet,
the cold gets into her
anyway,
running in slowly,
like a drip infusion,
spreading to throat, chest and ear,
it's winter here,
here in the heart of Holloway.

Messenger

A barrow of flames.
They're burning leaves
outside Saint Joseph's
Monastery. At the cross,
cars are trying to lick
their way out onto Highgate Hill.
The accelerator trembles under my feet,
rain comes down the window,
trays of water pushed flat
on each side by the wipers.
And down on the Holloway Road
an armoured biker
searches on the ground
beside his crashed bike,
his helmeted head
like a man from the future.
Or the past.
Lost.

The Air

In the beginning, I kept seeing fire
in the trees, every green lime
held a crimson fiery core,
a secret glowing lantern
in the high blue air.

Now, on Dartmouth Park Hill,
the leaves are gone yellow,
bundles of syrup coloured
rags lifting up and down,
in the high blue air.

Two Passionist Fathers come out
of the monastery. They've got
red hearts stitched on the outside
of their black breasts.
I feel the old fist in my throat again,
November's drawing in, I read it
in the high blue air.

Satsumas

I can rub away the skin
on your fat bellies with my thumb.
It's so easy. Pierce your fat
pumped up crescents with my teeth,
so the juice bursts sharp
on the peak of my tongue.
I never catch the taste,
it goes quick in a strong
orange smelling spray
that travels right to the top
of my nose and soaks my fingers,
until my skin is pain of orange.
And I rub your bellies all night,
like a murderer,
gone mad with the smell of her prey.

To Toblerone

Keats spoke of honeyed indolence,
I speak of Toblerone.
Running my finger over the brown
spine of many triangles,
I bite and look into the cliff
of chocolate that's left behind.
A castle of taste slides in
the moat of my mouth.
Shifting sweetness and brownness,
catching nougat against my teeth,
I straighten the silver paper out,
I stare down the barrel of the
red lettered triangular box,
and crash back on my cushions
like a mahogany pyramid,
like a Toblerone.

Missing Mountains

The curved load on the horizon,
pillowy puffs, five months pregnant.
Purple, green, brown, steamy blue,
not daring, not proud, just matronly bosoms,
Knockbrack, Knuttery, Nagle, Boggeragh,
Cusan, Wicklow, Magillacuddy.
Foggy breasts heaving and cleaving
into the rain loving sky. Half blown
balloons, in colours of earth and ocean,
bobbing and ducking in the mist.

The Plain Speaker

Petrol flames, blue and canary
billow between
the blades of my back,
temper tubes light up
and join wrist to elbow
knee to hip,
white iron arms
swell and crackle
when you have to *Put it Plain*
and *Say it Straight*.
My head flares like a beacon,
giving vent
from the blackened chimneys
of my smoking trunk.
You've managed to get
your knuckles in again.
Of course you find it painful.
Of course it's for my good.
But you do look happy,
your tongue is in the root.

Not Rumpelstiltskin

Ask the glass, or the cards will tell you.
Yes, you could go that way too,
you're on the right road if you turn around.
Guess his name. Try shining the dim light

from her torch into every creaking corner.
Is it Timothy, Ichabod, Benjamin or Jeremiah?
The moon between the curtains like the ball
in her hands when she tells you to concentrate.

Is it Bandy Legs, Hunchback or Crookshanks?
Jumping awake at every jangle, your nerves rapping
scared in your hollow yearning chest.
Is it Long Legs, Thin Waist or Generous Mouth?

And all the while at the back of the dance hall,
the dusky strains of music are jigging, *Round about,*
round about, Lo and behold! Reel away, reel away,
Straw into Gold.

It's not Rumpelstiltskin, smoking grass, or magic shoes,
it's not black hair, blue eyes or Tipperary accents.
The answer beats hard in your heart , girl,
but you don't want to be told.

Section 4:

"Love set you going like a fat gold watch."
Sylvia Plath

Labour in October

After the Paraclete
had blown me
from Holloway
to Crouch End Hill
and in the door
of the Anglican
church,
I stopped in the
porch to take the
damp cinnamon smell.

But Lo! The sound of a
hoover buffeted me back
and pink red apples
burst under my
feet
as I went again
a raw fish
and tramping the season
of ripe fruit
with our late baby
fastened in the rucksack
of my womb.

Winter's Grip

The rust leaved tree
was a torch, scorching
the brazen blue sky,
time for Persephone to go,
when white clouds crept,
and gripped the sky icily
a warning of the winter of
Demeter.

After your delicately
ripped red apple birth
a barren earth menaced,
showing how easily
from the dark below
the biscuit baby breath
could be snuffed
from you
carefully swaddled
mortal child.

Falling

Falling
in love
many times every
day this
long time
seven days seven since
you came out,
snuffling on the breast,
paper skin scented with
spice bouquet
blue eyes setting
out on another journey
another life's whorl
tasting, smelling, feeling me,
seeing each other for
long lasting moments,
you,
waving your legs
wrapped in toffee nappies.

Sleep

Asleep,
little corpse,
waxy,
death mask face
raised up
like a lamb
to the heavens,
I catch my breath
to hear her
tissue whisper breaths.

This Passion

I opened your wizard's jacket
with red and yellow stars,
loosened your face from
the green hood
your hands went wide like
the start of a blessing
and pulled, furious fingers
on my blouse, as I ached for
your touch, yet moved back.
Zipper quick was your hand
round my waist, taking
up the position, mouth caving
towards me.
Still brave, I shielded my body,
gasped, *Take this!* as I put
the orange juice to your lips.

They call this passion, weaning.

Separating

A bright tablet
framed
in the window,
sister moon
lights us
up the stairs.
Each creaking
tiptoe sets
a step
loudly groaning.
I shoulder
the small infant
her slack gut
mouth jutting
to the left,
one finger
still looped
in the curl
of my earring.
Ravines roar
in the wood.
Timber crack
shots burst
at the ball
of each foot,
as I feel
the cusp
of each stair
with my hopeful
stockinged sole.
At the cot,
I lever her down.
Slowly.

And go to my room
with a warm sticky print
branded on the right side
of my face and chest.

Wake

At the door
my rugged shadow
looms,
that's love
coming to wake you up.
With awkward tread,
heavy and wild,
I stare down at you,
pure putto,
with skin like soap
your balled up body
yawning itself out,
hands coming up
to cling, as we mash
our moist foreheads together.

Knitting

You sleep heavy,
chalk cheek pressed
against the sofa,
the other flame cheek
raised up to the light.
After this cranky
crying evening,
when irritable
and tooth driven
you made us long
for your silence,
we miss you already.
I touch the crease
where your wrist will be,
and press my lips against
your salt-sharp crown,
wishing
that I was a good knitter.
I'd make a grand blue canopy,
purled with stars and cabled moons,
then I'd buy a packet
of four fat Italian cherubs
to hold it up
over the cot
in your room.

Insomnia

She was Shakespearean about sleep,
with wild hollow looks at the mirror,
her grey face chanted over us,
Not a wink, not a wink, one, two,
three o' clock, don't talk to me
about suffering, four, five, six o' clock,
when I heard Mikey Dorgan's churns
I knew I was finished.
Macbeth could talk about knitting
up the sleeve of care,
Henry the Fourth could talk
about Nature's soft nurse,
but she had been nurse and knitter
to ten children. Sleep was the gold
always slipping through her fingers,
because she didn't know
that she really was sleeping,
she was unconscious while we crashed
and tossed on the sea of her sorrowful snores.

Líadain's Gloves

Summer Witch has grabbed the country,
nails drip dark red on the fuschia,
blue cloak flares over purple hills,
white roses frill the savage pricks.
Mist descends, and the cows stand in
by the ditch, while rain anoints the window.
Líadain slips a foxglove on to each tiny fat finger.
Is it digitalis that rocks our heartbeats down
to the movement of a big slow clock?
We need no help clambering on to the giant dial,
she heaves herself onto my chest, then lies
perspiring, heavy in my arms.

Blue Frost Moon

The moon is reflecting
the sun's gold with pure silver,
it's a round full drop sitting
high in our tall blue windows.

She doesn't mind the cold,
climbing onto a chair
in front of the dressing table.
She's looking at her face.

Outside the orange lamp
is sitting in the branches
of a bare apple tree,
turning the apples copper.

She holds an egg green compact,
snapping it open and shut,
flashing bits of my eyes, nose
and forehead into my face.
She's calling me by my first name.

The copper apples are like something
out of a fairy tale, like Christmas trees.

She's standing between the curtains,
snapping her mirror at the window.
She wants the moon to look at itself.
Moon, moon, I hear her calling.

Section 5:

Like a coloniser

Gale

There's a gale around this
gold grey building,
gothic points
enter an angel blue sky.
On the inside, the wind
is a demon, rattling glass
and Victorian brick,
raging tremendously
down voluminous corridors.
Death slants, the old lie,
tubed and bored. All except Lily
thrown down on her wheeled
throne, face vivacious,
talking to the air above
her voluptuous
rotting
leg.

Ward A 11

The wind stood outside
and roared in the window,
They tried to tighten the latch
but it came in anyway,
keen to be going down
the old wards, where
the dead lay dying.
It sliced the nurses'
pale blue dresses
and flattened the beards
of the porters, as they
wheeled the steel coffin
through that snaky twine of air.
A wanton meanderer,
describing eerie wheels.
Their lives in the middle,
unwinding.

Barium Swallow

On the screen, the skeleton
knocks the dense liquid
back through its grinning mouth,
mad and bad looking,
like a pirate's flag.

The woman herself swallows
nervously, unable to follow
the instructions properly,
she smells of talcum powder
and strawberry flavoured Barium.

Air is black and bone is white,
somewhere in between is risk.
Judgement will be drawn from these shadows,
and negative and positive will matter
even though the skeleton is already plotted out.

There's a Snake in my Back

There's a snake
in my back,
he spreads his poison
like a stain, pouring
liquid fire
into my sacrum.
Ropy, hard, and unrepentant
it's six years since
he slithered in
yanked my neck,
as the car jerked,
disturbing
the beaded bone string
of my human spine.
Now it belongs
to devil's assistant,
he rears and tears
along the bone
lying quiet
in the doctor's waiting room,
his dark eyes
liquid evil,
winking through the eyes
of my sacrum,
his narrow head
laughing,
flipping
his tail,
telling
his cervical,
thoracic
lumbar rosary down
to my coccyx, until
the seventh year when
I finally get his measure.
This year,
I'll get a priest
to say a prayer
or a witch doctor
to fry a chop,
use money,
buy him out of the bone.

Ghosts

Under the ocean of an old hospital,
lie the silted remains
of an X-ray department.
Generators clog with dust,
thick pipes coil and clamp
across couches. Brown wooden grids,
marked in squares divided by black crosses,
control panels vomiting their guts
of blue, red, and yellow filaments.
Here kilovolts were generated,
current over time
blackening the shadowy pictures
stolen from where blood flowed
between bone, heart and lung.
On a shelf of grey blue tiles,
livers, brains, kidneys,
muscles flattened like seaweed,
the long strand of a spinal cord,
foetuses trapped in alcohol.
Under glass, Siamese twins
throw chalky arms around each other.
They're not waving,
their mouths are open, gasping,
they're not breathing.

Revision of a Hip Replacement

Compression plates, buttress plates,
capenet gouge, pidcock punch.
A body thrown up on its side,
split right open on the flank,
swathes of red muscle glisten,
this hip is to be fixed.

Tommy bar, Lempert's elevator,
box spanners, bone cutters.
The surgeon drives the drill,
a mad motor cycle man,
with flecks of blood and fat on his visor.
He shouts, we jump, he's important.

The drawers are filled with sterilised equipment,
carefully labelled, nibblers, knee spreaders,
Watson Cheyne Probe, patties. The body is groaning,
he drives the drill, like a coloniser.

The fat is flying, you'd like to wipe his sneer, but it's
mole wrench, Bennett's cobra head, broken screw removing kit.
Enough words for a book of psalms, enough sulks for Jehovah.
Norwich retractor, tenotomy knife, Allen keys, humphy skid.
Angels of reconstruction can afford to be fiery.

Good Killers

Surgeons would make good killers,
they're used to cutting great grinning
wounds through fat packed close
like crimson worms. The limp frame
is flung down, they don't mind
worrying it with tube and drill
and prising gloved fingers deep
into the red secrets
of the body. This body which is
just as likely to jump up and shout
Hi! Stop! as any corpse
flattened on the floor.

Crocodile

The X-ray lady had yellow and white badges shaking on her dress
and metal things were making a noise in her pocket.

Shelley, I need to take some pictures of your arms,
your legs, your back and chest, can you take
off your dress for me?

They made Mummy wait in the ward, her pretend smile was
dropping down.
She kept saying that I wasn't to talk about Daddy.

Shelley, there's nothing to worry about, slip off your dress.

A fat grey crocodile hung out of the back of the machine,
it groaned when she pulled it across the room.

Shelley, let me undo the zip at the back!

Another X-ray lady came in and looked at me. She said that there
were chests waiting, but she'd bang them off in room six.
The crocodile swung his scabby tail.

Shelley, what age are you? Did you say six?

My X-ray lady was getting worry men in her eyes like Mummy.

It's only your dress, Shelley.

The crocodile was going green and fatter, she wanted me to lie
under it. I held my dress next to my neck.

I'll help you, Shelley, it's just the zip that's in the way of
your picture.

The crocodile was starting to groan again, sometimes he hummed and he made the machine go click, click, click.

Shelley, let me, gently, here at the back.

Crocodile was rising, but she couldn't see him coming, humming and clicking, his red lights turned on. *I've banged those off,* said the other lady.

Please, Shelley! said the X-ray lady and the worry men ran all over her eyes.

Section 6.

" Come then, royal girl and royal times,
Come quickly,
I can be happy until you come
But I cannot be heavenly,
Only disenchanted people
Can be heavenly."

Stevie Smith
The Frog Prince, 1966

Like an Angel from Below

I first saw him,
walking along the road to Dromard,
pure wicked, like an angel from below.

On a grey road, beside a moss ditch,
under branches of blackthorn he stood,
staring with treacly eyes.

He stopped me, with only a few words
and I can't remember them, it was his
eyes that had me.

He touched the sleeve of my coat,
I was only twelve, but he made me
feel woman.

I wanted to touch his hair, black
and stiff, pushing down over the collar
of his coat.

He told me he knew my sister,
and I was afraid of that even then, afraid
of the knowledge.

I first saw Justin on the Dromard Road,
he had me with his eyes, black eyes,
black as the tar on the road. Pure wicked
like an angel from below.

The Blank Map

The Master's hair is Brillo, his eyes streak malice,
he's waiting for me to talk. I'm sure that I won't this time.
His eyes are filling green. Third class are up.
Looking stupid in front of the blank map.
He likes surprising us, terrifying us, unrolling
that fat emerald naked lion body of Ireland.

Would you be familiar with the source of the Shannon, Miss D?
Perchance, you'd show it to us? Tongue whittling
the inside of his cheek. Suppressing diabolical laughter.
Miss D looks back at me. The Master's eyes fly to my face.
I twirl my compass. Miss D's fingers quiver in Leinster
and then move to the North. I know that it isn't there. I try
to shake my head invisibly.

Miss D, you're moving dangerously close to Belfast!
Will you settle there, you stupid oinseach?
No sir, no sir, moans Miss D. *Or do you know anything?*
The Master thrusts his face close. Spittle.
I do, Sir, I do, Sir. Miss D holds the coloured marker,
Bends her face to mine again. His breathing quickens
as he watches me. I shake my head more visibly.
His narrow grey skull darts up with relief.

Miss Boylan, how many more times do I have to tell you to stop
talking?

Radiance is on his face, at last he can run to his creaking
desk, fumble for his sweet supple ash stick. Rain down singing
whirrs on the tips of our red fingers.

Afterwards, he's triumphant. Thrusting us to our seats.
We've got pink and blue woollen tents sitting on our shoulders
from where he's pulled us around by our cardigans.
Our hands sting, they're huge strange things, pulsing in our
laps.

Miss Boylan, how many more times do I have to tell you to stop talking?

I'm afraid it's forever. For life. He grins. He's so pleased.
I look at the inkwells, they are white top hats.
The Master's favourite is filling them, slowly, carefully,
with dark blue ink.

The Curse

An angel was stirring my stomach,
with an iron spoon, "I'll never
get over this!" I pitched
into the bed with my eyes closed.

I know all about suffering, she said
and lowered herself in beside me.
Not a month passed when I wasn't
laid low, if anyone asks what's wrong
with you, tell them your aunt is visiting.

She got in and out of the bed, came in
and out with hot water bottles, told me
that it was in my blood to suffer.

Pale roses swam on the carpet, the wallpaper stepped
in and out until the lurid light died through
the orange curtains and I sat drinking iced water.
It's over! we cried and the slice of lemon
in the glass bumped against my lips like a frog.

Nancy's Mirror

That's where the backcombing and the eyeshadow
gets you! My mother didn't say this to Nancy's face,
and she said that she was sorry for her really.
It took me a while to work out what was going on,
Father Hare giving advice inside in the pantry,
Mick hissing, saying that Nancy was no angel.
My mother packing Nancy's case for England,
exchanging regal looks with the three oval mirrors,
that swivelled and framed Nancy's dressing table.

The three mirrors had watched the backcombing,
I watched too, climbing into her iron bed,
shrouding myself in her white bedspread.
Nancy's arms used to ache at first,
teasing out each strand.
The hiss and fizz of the hairspray,
sometimes she let me press the nozzle,
shower her dark hair with glistening drops.

Nancy's two sisters stood in the side mirrors,
Nodding, lifting and dropping their arms together.
Nancy's right side was different from her left.
Nancy thought her right side was awful.
Like Montgomery Clift, she wouldn't show it to the camera.
Sometimes there were too many faces, making me queasy.
I could only look at the middle Nancy,
painting her face with red and brown and blue.

And then black, sharp on her eyes and eyebrows,
tissue between her lips to dampen the red a bit,
winking at my pale young face that appeared
in the background like a ghost,
just like Nancy's was now,
pale and queer, hair lying down lazy.
Bottles of Carling Black Label,

Consulate cigarettes. All her colours gone,
standing in her beautiful lacy slip
looking at her stomach in the mirrors,
holding it in, looking at it from the side.
Looking.

Dyeing

Branches knocked on the window
rain lashed itself around the house,
and crept under the door,
as if it was making a go for Teresa.
Nancy dipped the metal hook through
Teresa's mesh hat, selecting hairs
for Peroxide. Teresa was nervous.

Mick threw open the back door,
ran in with a brown sack.
A bit of the wild night came in with him,
made him bawl under his stormy hair,
pour whiskey into a mug, pour it into his mouth,
pour rain drenched kittens on the table,
their dead faces stiff.

I went out into the night, crying for the kittens,
went down to Justin's caravan, let him take off
my wet clothes, let him take me under the covers.
Afterwards it didn't seem the comfort
I'd hoped for. When I got back,
Teresa Sheehy's hair
had gone irreparably yellow.

Loves' Kitchen

I was playing 21 in Loves' kitchen,
when Justin sat down beside me,
his stiff hair,
his brown fingers around the ace,
his long legs.

Justin sat down beside me,
started talking to Violet Love,
his big mouth teasing,
her high voice lifting,
her flowery breasts rising.

They said it was time I went to bed,
that my mother would be worried,
Violet's clucking,
Justin's eyes,
and me, raging and smiling my tears.

He got up to get my coat,
helped put me into it,
Violet poking red coals,
Justin slipping his jacket,
coming with me.

The trees waved us forward,
sweeping us with black bending shadows,
his hand, my hand,
the moon a silver cut,
my heart lapping.

Her Lesson

Nancy was back from England
with a flat stomach, a mustard skirt
and a curl on each cheek.

She said that she'd lost it.
They said that she'd got away with murder
that she hadn't learnt her lesson.

But she had learnt to inhale, to blow
the smoke carelessly past her fringe,
to make chilli con carne,
to say *Fuck this for a game of soldiers!*
to smile when her heart leaked.

Dear Mother

Dear Mother,
he came with his black hair and his purple jacket.
He was so graceful, even walking over stones.

Mick said that Justin walked like he'd a hurley shoved up his
arse, but what did Mick know? He was always falling over bits
of rusty machinery and his own two feet.

Highwayman's breeches, hooves on the road. Hazelnuts,
chocolate, Malt and Cream toffees.

My eyes fixed on his hands, moving on me.

His hardness inside me, pushing. Better than a whole ton
of chocolate and nuts.

And I always let him back, even when you could light the
whiskey air around him.

Dear Mother, you'll never read these letters.